SENSITIVITY

Poems of a Highly Sensitive Teenager.

Any Pascual

Copyright © 2023 Any Pascual

All rights reserved

No part of this book may be reproduced, or stored in a retrieval system, or transmitted in any form or by any means, electronic, mechanical, photocopying, recording, or otherwise, without express written permission of the publisher.

ISBN: 9798871531808

Cover design by: Priscila Do Amaral Gibert.

"Poetry is the feeling that is left over from the heart and comes out of your hand." (1)

CARMEN CONDE. DICTIONARY OF QUOTATIONS.

To all the Highly Sensitive People in the world.
And to Dr. Elaine Aron,
researcher of the trait.
To those who have not yet been born,
and to those who don't know (yet) they are.
Because I want to tell your story,
which is also mine
and that of many more
who are like us.
Because we are valuable,
because we are HSP.

To all those who have lost touch
with their sensitive hearts.
And to everyone who won
love,
respect
and acceptance.

To my parents.
And to you, reader,
because the purpose
of this book
is to help you
connect with who you are,
to understand
ourselves and yourself
in the message
that is conveyed
everywhere,
in all the verses
that are written
and in each of the rhymes
of these numerous poems:
Sensitivity should not be a curse,
when it's really a great condition.

Any Pascual.

CONTENTS

Title Page
Copyright
Epigraph
Dedication

Sensitivity.	1
Driving through life.	3
705 more words on sensitivity.	8
If I could...	13
12 verses of propensity.	15
Traveler.	16
Grandmother.	17
Ode to Plaza Cibeles.	21
January 31st.	23
Haiku to my mother.	27
The past shapes us.	28
Short and slight poem.	30
Wind, what I feel.	31
My home.	33
Terminal haiku.	34

Just what you need.	35
L-O-V-E.	36
Mother's Day (haiku).	37
Free energy.	38
Thoughtful haiku at sunset.	39
Today, being your birthday.	40
Heat wave.	42
Haiku in memory.	43
400 words about both sides of sensitivity.	44
Release.	47
Because.	48
My congratulation (first part).	50
New season.	51
Haiku of the book.	53
A book to teach me to…	54
Silence.	56
My congratulation (extension).	57
Verses.	60
Haiku of new beginnings.	62
Verbosity felt at dawn.	63
Uplifting haiku.	65
Poetry.	66
Cycles.	68
December 3rd.	69
Events of the moment.	75
Why I sigh.	76

Reserve poem.	77
Imported and determined.	78
For my guardian angel.	80
Haiku to the rainbow.	87
Strength.	88
Christmas for me.	89
Hours of sleep.	91
I wish…	92
Too long-awaited endings.	99
These walls cry out your name.	101
Bonus	103
Joy of being.	104
Too much wind.	107
Summary of you and me.	109
Haiku of hope.	111
Platonic.	112
I think so.	120
On her day, for my mother.	122
Safe and sound.	123
Güelito.	125
Fear.	127
Authenticity.	130
Acknowledgements.	137
About The Author	147
Books By This Author	149
Author's Notes	151

SENSITIVITY.

Sensitivity.
A reality.

Sensitivity should not be a curse,
when it's really a great condition.

Sensitivity is a journey.
Something in which, sometimes, we need guidance.

Many times we look for answers in the ordinary world.
A world that often doesn't get how it feels to be a sensitive person.

It simply is life seen differently.
From other eyes, feeling deeply.

There is nothing weird about us, we are more than twenty percent of those people who have a mind.

The lights, the noise, the hustle and bustle
appear to us as an annoying symphony.

We perceive things that others can't see,

and I ask myself, "Why do't they try to understand?"

Emotions for us are like a sea
in which we can either sink or sail.

We tend to avoid the crowds
and in silence we'd like to take refuge.

DRIVING THROUGH LIFE.

Driving through life.

I wish I knew the answers
inside,
could stop being afraid
and go roaring out into the center lane
until I park at home.
I wish that emotions
could simply warn.
It would be useful to know,
don't you agree?
If there was a sign that said
"A wave of anger is coming".
And maybe something to stop me
long before I get to grief.
I would like a handbrake
to put the joy on pause.
Because if I step on the gas
it turns itself
(too soon, too fast),
without being able to stop it,

into apathy.
I wish I could change lanes
when dissatisfaction
nears
by exceeding the speed limits.
I'd be happy if I could stop
my emotions from controlling me,
if the temperature
of my body vehicle
didn't keep me frozen
even when I open the hood.
I'd like to see something
through the dirty
windshield
of routines.
I wish my retinas
allowed me to look
in the rearview mirror,
but I drive
my life,
my body,
my world,
and unfortunately
I cannot look away
(even for a second)
to see what's around me.
I would like to find
in peace
my spare wheel.
But I dare not
go to the rear.
I dare not make changes,
not even for good news.

SENSITIVITY

I don't know if there's anyone else
in this car.
What I do know is
that I have to be careful.
I cannot overreach,
not even slow down.
I haven't taken a turn
for two years
and I haven't stopped
for three summers now.
I am not going to take
this metaphor any further,
I'll just make a couple of analogies.
The last time I ventured
into the trunk,
I found only memories,
nightmares,
broken things,
and knives.
So I know
I can't stop,
because fear follows me
and it's almost caught me up.
And you may wonder
Why don't I decide to speed up,
run,
and leave everything behind?
Well, you see,
it's because this car
was born
with a factory
defect.
Well,

several,
because sometimes the engine
stops working
and expels
with difficulty
something that's not right in there.
But the main defect
is much more imperfect.
And that affects everyone
and all along the way,
every mile
traveled
and every person
who gets in here with me.

I am responsible for every life,
for every inch,
for my destiny.
I can't let us
collide,
I can't let myself get discouraged.
I can't afford to give up.
If there really is someone here
by my side,
or behind me,
there is no one I
can
pass
control to.
And I can't just fail
because, you see
(you better know by now):
this car

SENSITIVITY

doesn't have
seat belts.

705 MORE WORDS ON SENSITIVITY.

Although some more, all human beings feel.
Those who do the most are us, a fifth of humanity.

Have you ever seen a prism,
one of those that turn white light into color?

I believe that we the HSP are like this;
we transform and sense everything that affects us.

There are others, "lightly",
who can control their "slightly" sensitive... mind.
They all are part of another percentage, twenty
who can
empathize with those who are different.
More than the remaining sixty percent.

In that group of the "other" twenty
who, like us, feel more than usual,
is my blessed mother, by choice or by luck.

That is the environment where sensitivity is loved,
cherished,

accepted
and perhaps even actively cultivated.

We HSP also grow up in challenging places,
where they ask us, "Where the hell are you today?!"
every time we say, "Why don't you feel more?"

The point here is that we cannot control
the degree to which things will affect us.

What we can do is to be aware
and be as we are, always consistent.

Some of us can't endure the ceiling lights
and for others, a perfume can cause them to flee.

For many, books are the best peers
because they are what we want,
without being too extreme.

Going to a concert is normally a torture
(unless it's classical music, then it results in good fortune)
and trying a board game, a version of adventure.

Most of us cannot stand loud noises
and we are typically more patient.

Some suffer with huge anxiety;
most of us are just looking for love and tranquility.

It is not so difficult to recognize us,
just reach out with love and try to understand us.

We are very affected by physical pain,
so try to avoid a critical point.

We're good at listening
and, myself included, we'd like to be talking.

The best thing for us is to reduce stimulation
and almost always calm our internal emotion.

Sometimes we wish we were normal.
I give thanks that we are more than animals.

Some of us feel what the other person feels...
More HSPs still isolate themselves to not notice everything so much.

Some of us have extrasensory abilities,
others often ask themselves existential questions.

I belong to both, and that's why I write sensitive poems.
To communicate how the world is perceived by me.

Many of us have obsessions,
and we are very, completely happy
when expanding,
expressing,
exploring,
allowing ourselves to be captivated,
transformed,
with our whole heart and soul loving
and time (hopefully this entire life) dedicating
to art, feelings,

memories,
emotions
and passions.

The way you behave soothes or stresses us.
And on many occasions, living our life weighs us down.

How can you calm our inner self?
What works for me is to write and meditate.

Sometimes HSPs are either mature or childish.
Some advice! Never call us "shy".
Not all of us fit into those profiles.

Actually, we almost always want to love,
it just happens that we are afraid to speak
(or rather, of how people will react)
or, in many cases, that we don't know how to express ourselves.

To conclude,
or almost,
I want to apologize to sensitive men
for everything they have had to go through in the West
and also for always using the female gender.
I consider myself and was born a woman,
and HSP stands for Highly Sensitive People, that's right.
So forgive me, sensitive man, if you read me;
I do and will generalize the trait as feminine.

Now, 593 words later, I want to finish
with this: never will everything be said about sensitivity,
so this poetry book I will keep on writing.

These messages from my poems I want you to take home:
feeling more does not have to be a reason for sorrow.
I vibrate at the frequency of a world where sensitivity
is synonymous with love, peace and happiness.
Because I want to live in a place where it is plausible
that society accommodates highly sensitive people.

By the time you finish reading me, I want you to have this choice:
Sensitivity should not be a curse,
when it's really a great condition.

NOTE 2.

IF I COULD...

*Dedicated to my father, my mirror,
a (not very) mature being. Thanks for inspiring me.*

If I could contort my body,
I would, I assure you.
If I could go back into my own story,
I would, even if I don't last.
If I could command my time,
I would, even if it's hard.
If I could direct my element,
I would, even if I break against a wall.
If I could color this moment,
I would, even if it's dark.
If I could harmonize my thinking,
I would, maybe that way I heal.
If I could live writing...
If I could write everything while living...
I would do it, no doubt, with a single dollar.
If I could fully remember those days, and those nights,
believe me, I would, with a charm.

If I could...

If I could choose what I feel...
No, I wouldn't, it would be subverting a pure knack.

I would...
If I could grow in love knowing...
Would I, having to lose you...? I swear?

12 VERSES OF PROPENSITY.

Because I love you
and I don't want to hide it.
I want to share it!

For I yearn for you
and I don't want to avoid it.
I want to say it!

Since I'm looking for you,
I'm not going to deny it.
I'm going to write it!

Today I crave
and I will not deprive myself.
I imagine us.

TRAVELER.

Hello.
Are you lost?
Or do you not even
know that there is a road?

Let me show you my verses;
may they serve as your compass,
traveler.

GRANDMOTHER.

«For you, grandmother, from your granddaughter...»

Grandmother,
of life experience a great school.

I know, because you told me,
that you don't want me to thank you.
Days ago you were talking about a show with locusts,
and I couldn't help but think
as I heard you talking about it:
"You are great! Thank you, because you opened your house to us."

In it, a long time ago, you lived with us for a few years,
and you allowed us to change your way of eating and cooking.

The strength of your heart is such, your love so big,
that our weirdness you endure with great spirit.

Servir y proteger
is a TV show you like to watch.

And I, your only granddaughter, know
that this is
what I've always seen you do with us.
You do it because you love us,
so much that you have several photos
of me
in the bookshelf.

Over many months,
you endured our many stresses.
You give us your time every time we visit you
and you love your family with all your soul.

Your mother, Peregrina, had a fiery temper,
and she gave you her big, beautiful heart.
You take care of us like a mother bear.
In your past, that I hear, there is something new and precious.

When I embrace you, I feel
warmth, peace, security and a loving feeling
that I cannot find the words to describe,
but that I can feel with you every day.
Even if I know that you need to rest from our presence,
I want you to know that your girl will love you
(and remember).
You used to tell my mother "pretty, ugly",
and that tradition passed on to us, funny.
Now you and I say "fashion, beauty".
When I think about it, I understand that I love you, all of you.

You have eyes full of curiosity

that convey to anyone what is in you,
an unlimited and generous kindness.
Your small mouth allows me to notice
(accurately)
that more than speaking, you are a person who knows how to listen.

You have shown (I heard it well, each year) many times your character,
you are also firm and persistent.

(Even that you got from your mother.)

I appreciate
that anything you buy for me is priceless.
Now I can cherish
the evenings telling me about your family, about your village by the sea.
Thank you for being there when we need you
and for asking us every day how we are.

I am absolutely sure that Cándido is proud of you
watching how you treat us when we are here and there,
five hundred and eighty-six miles from your life,
and seeing your way of loving and feeling.

I love you, *Güelita*,
since the very first day.
Asturian woman, from Bañugues,
you have in your blood your sincere personality.

I understand that you will always see me as
"the most beautiful girl in the world",

and I accept it.
With this poem I've wanted to summarize what I feel for you.

Though we rarely see in person,
and we barely tell each other,
we love each other very much,
like trout to *troutess*.

NOTE 3.

ODE TO PLAZA CIBELES.

Today the sun shines on your painting.
And every time I passed by your side
I remember, close to the Prado.

That never-named artist
painted you like a queen in her reign.

And now I regret not
having given you my attention.

One minute, for an emotion.
Perhaps evoking a song.

Being in your city and not going,
being another, would be like not living.

But at least I can appreciate you
and create, about you, art.

Being close I get overwhelmed
But now I want to touch your wall.

Because you are pretty, and now I can feel
what for so many years I could not perceive.

After almost a decade of yearning,
and at the same time rejecting...

Going to see your cultural beauty
because it seemed terminal to me.

Something from a time I didn't love,
and therefore disdained.

Now I lament
not having given in to the torment
I thought was going to see your structure,
when you radiate so much loveliness.

In the hotel, in silence,
I thank you for this feeling.
Thank you, expression of architecture.
Thank you, of my ancient pure city.

Thank you, monument!
Great place of the new city council.

Thank you, Cybele.
To the goddess and to the painting of honey.

JANUARY 31ST.

2019, January, 31st.
I finish a chapter of my story almost at midnight.
At 23:30 I write this:
These are some plane tickets.

It was the moment when I really made up my mind.
I knew I wanted not to design, but to write.

When I put my finger on the button *publish*,
I finished something that I didn't know how many times to revise.

I spent ten hours that day without stopping
transcribing messages that manage to move me.

Many months later, I realized my mistake.
No family to write, later was a horror.

On the other hand, on the emotional side,
every word I wrote was vital.

When I finished, I went to sleep satisfied
because that part of my purpose was fulfilled.

I typed at full speed.
And even so, I think, with my characteristic quality.

I wanted to congratulate my best friend there,
because she was turning sixteen and she also supports me here.

And with the confidence
that generates a fair self-praise,
I fell asleep and don't know what I dreamed,
although I am sure I rested.

It was the end of a belief,
and the beginning of thousands of experiences.

Because besides liking it so,
then I understood that is what I can dedicate myself to.

January 31st, 2020.
I still have pending the end of my story.
This morning began with the realization
of how far this account has come in a year.

When I woke up I had a lot of overactivation,
and that's why I gave myself attention.

Thanks to the silence I easily meditated,
and started the day well because I calmed down.

Then, true to my pagan faith, I prayed
and to those I trust I offered food.

SENSITIVITY

As I had bread with tomato for breakfast,
I spoke peacefully with my family.

The slice of tomato I served myself
had angel wings on it, I saw.

That it was a good omen I trusted,
because it was in my visions, as I realized.

I wanted to learn what was beautiful in the world today,
and that's why I went to Instagram.

Because social media filters information
and, if we know how to use it, avoids overstimulation.

Minutes later I moved back
to what I was doing a year ago.

And because of that, this poem grows
to express the past that returns.

And what I did next I do not remember,
maybe because it's something I don't really feel.

I simply live life,
trying not to let sensitivity define me.

It does whether we like it or not,
and I understood that for the worst.

This afternoon mixed emotions,
caused by familiar disputes.
"Familiar" in both meanings;
in both it implies strong feelings.

Hours of reading and other activities
that are no longer singular...

...

At 6:30 p.m., seeking to recover the past,
the quiet time was officially over.

That will be another poem...
...dealing with a recurring theme.

I summarize it in two verses,
now that I have it fresh:
Why does ever-recurrent bad health
complicate doing what my soul feels?

Guilt came out of my eyes,
and they ended up red.

I know it is the other side of the scale,
but there are days when it takes away my hope.

I know that an artistic sensitivity
may be associated with a medical illness.

Also, mine with these verses rhymes,
and that's a lot of me to unknown people.

What I want to say, HSP,
is that our body does not have to accompany.

If we don't allow it to express its state
it will ultimately make us sick and make us cry.

We can try to overcome our sensitivity,
but we must always remember our body.

HAIKU TO MY MOTHER.

Your eye, so profound,
takes me back to our household.
I love you lots, mom.

THE PAST SHAPES US.

What I do not trust
is people forgetting their past.
Because everyone who doesn't learn its lessons,
the ones who choose to live hiding
from what it can unfold,
are going to replay the game they lose
every time they start to change,
to get cocky
or to act like they're bold.
The people who don't learn from their path
are going to repeat what they are loath
to face,
many times in forms they loathe
with all their hearts.
Don't forget or dismiss your story.
Unless you want to make history
in every way possible,
and each worse than the last.
So, my advice is this:
Acknowledging your life may not help

solving it,
but it certainly doesn't hurt.
Not at all.

SHORT AND SLIGHT POEM.

"What are you looking at?" "Memories".
In the park next door
I see you again,
and memories of the past
return to the present.

WIND, WHAT I FEEL.

Wind (air) is the most powerful
of the four elements.

The wind...
The wind carries the ashes of the fire.
And without hesitation, it murmurs: "I move you...
... and wherever I want now I take you."
The wind shakes the flame of each candle,
guides it from left to right and freezes it.
The wind is like that, or the other way around,
it can be a soothing breeze, do you want it?
The wind can put out a blaze,
or it can spread and propagate it beyond repair.
The wind also blows away the wood
that the burning bonfire generates,
causing it to be lost without any delay.

The wind changes the (dis)course of the current.
And moves the waves of the sea, patient.
The wind changes the state of the water, intelligent.
The wind directs the rain, diligent.
The wind manipulates the river, sometimes impertinent.
The wind brings humidity, present...

The wind can also take it away, suddenly.

The wind can help, gently,
or it can destroy our home, such a reality.
The wind can generate hurricanes, and ferocity.
Or it can suggest realities, our curiosity.
The wind stirs up dust, what a calamity!
The wind can also heal us, a beauty.
The wind can break the walls, without iniquity.
The wind can bend the paper, what a sensitivity.

The wind, less dense than anything,
is mightier than water, fire and earth.

The wind is the vehicle of being.
The wind, my, our spirit,
the wind, the soul that you are,
like all that is essential, is invisible.
It is sensible, but not measurable...
(The wind,
the soul, sensitivity, what I feel...)
...is the source of love, it cannot be seen.

MY HOME.

Inspired by the style of Defreds (José Ángel Gómez Iglesias), and dedicated to Jorge Luis Iglesias, @JorgeIglesias1 on Wattpad. Sempiternal.

Most people
build their homes
using bricks or stone.

My home is made of love,
trust,
memories,
and stardust.

In that order.

Many people see in their houses only a place
to sleep;
For me, it is the best place to dream.

TERMINAL HAIKU.

It begins and ends.
That is the end of the good;
also of the bad.

JUST WHAT YOU NEED.

Sometimes,
seeing the world go on
for people,
when it hurts you to live,
is horrible.
But there are other times,
like this morning,
when it's just what you need.

L-O-V-E.

L-ight.
Be a light
in the life
of your loved one.

O-bservation.
Practice observation
to know
your true self,
and the true self of
your significant other.

V-alue.
Value your time together
and your differences.

E-mpathy.
Be empathetic
and respectful with
each and every being.

These are the key points of self
L-O-V-E.

MOTHER'S DAY (HAIKU).

Your soul and mine,
together forever, ma.
Today and always.

FREE ENERGY.

On the narrow margin
between fire and ice,
life fully emerges.

It (the world) is created
when a way
is found
to enter the deepest.

The expected
causes mechanisms;
the creative
generates
mirrors where we see ourselves.

THOUGHTFUL HAIKU AT SUNSET.

It has been months, six
now, since I saw you again
in my awakening.

TODAY, BEING YOUR BIRTHDAY.

5/17.

*For you, family,
especially for Héctor, on this his blessed day.
And also for Melodía.
Thank you for sending her to take care of me
when I don't find you here by my side,
when land and ocean separate us.
You already know: I hold you in my heart.*

Now I can say,
as I hear the blackbirds sing,
that I feel you close to me
and that I can now hug you.
Today I write here
because there's something to celebrate.
Six times twenty springs since your birth have just taken place
and this day is special, so it to you I will dedicate.
I love you with *storge*, I love all the truth that is about you.

I understand, and this afternoon I am learning to sing
to bring my family the happiness that it gives you, yes.

I saw you again crossing the bridge years ago, with those you love,
and I became once again, thanks to you, who I was when we hugged.

Thank you, Héctor, for months now we have been able to link both souls,
and I cherish talking, I want to stay with you and be, as I wrote, just like this.

HEAT WAVE.

Dedicated to my mother, who came up with the title of this short poem.

Early bird
needs to sleep
in order to evade
the intense heat.

HAIKU IN MEMORY.

In commemoration of the life, love and kindness that Chadwick Boseman has given to this world, and for him to continue to do so on the other side. Your soul is brilliant and has brightened thousands of lives, touched thousands of hearts forever. Thank you for being. Enjoy your existence, you deserve the best. Salve.

RIP in Elysium.
You are still loved, Panther King.
We remember you.

400 WORDS ABOUT BOTH SIDES OF SENSITIVITY.

For us, sensitivity is sometimes a jinx;
but that is because we do not understand the meaning of this gift.

Sensitivity, pain, reminds us that we are alive.
It is the best way to know that we have survived.

Many times we'd like to apply something on us to numb what we feel,
we want to avoid suffering, but without suffering the senses do not exist.

And if the senses do not exist,
there is no life,
there is no hope;
there is nothing
that makes us get up every morning.

Living is not easy, one suffers a lot.
Sometimes, we feel love for someone who really is not good, but a simple mongrel.
Sensitivity only makes that increase more:
there are reactions that, as much as we want
(and we want to),
we cannot change.

We can be very positive.
We can quiet our inner selves by becoming active.
We can carry out activities
that take our mind out of our realities.

But in the end, life will come back;
we cannot run forever from our pangs.

Sensitivity makes us take things from the heart;
the problem comes when these things have no solution.

Sensitivity is a very beautiful trait,
we can be happy just by listening to music or smelling a cake,
but sensitivity is like a rose:
if you look closely at it, the thorns will destroy you.

Sensitivity makes us make thousands of tiny mistakes;
constantly, we live life passing through disappointments.

Sensitivity makes us avoid conflicts,
but we almost always cause them ourselves.

Living with other HSPs is complicated.

With those who are not, Oops, altercations are expected!

When we have relaxing moments, we can appreciate our inner wonder.
But, I confess, that's almost never a given.
There are few moments in life when it is deeply pleasurable to feel.
And books don't prepare us to live together; they don't get us out of there.
I admit that many times we need to explode,
although the things we do it for seem to matter to none.

I admit that, many days,
my sensitivity has been where I got lost.
I still lose my temper if there's confrontation.

I admit that my sensitivity is a burden to be normal, someone who can live doing.
I admit that I only feel safe without acting, without changing, just existing.

And yes, I can say without fear of being wrong
that also me, during that time I'm in my heels,
this sensitivity that I value loads and heaps
I begin and end hopelessly hating and cursing.

RELEASE.

I let go, I am;
broken glass dreams
were realized today.

BECAUSE.

Because the truth is
that if the consequences of saying
"I love you"
make us see the world burn,
it suits me,
because there are reasons and reasons,
hundreds of.
And if no one else dares to be,
I don't care if I have to burn it
myself,
because we will be free,
and we will survive.
Because, you know, my inner demons
tell me that I can't let
it end,
let you cease,
there be accidents
or me not to get up,
unforeseen.
Because I-I'm afraid of you,
like that, like babbling.
Because I'm like that baby
who doesn't know if her mother is going to return

when she can no longer
touch her with the tips of her...
feelings.
Because every time
I go offline
(every time I detach),
I don't know if you'll come back.
I don't know whether the yets, the stills,
the wants, the I wish,
and the love that's flawless and perfect
will be back.
Because if a world burns for
loving ourselves,
that's better than a world without affection,
dead.
Because, with all the whys
and what I appreciate in life,
what I have learned is that
the consequences of telling you
that I love you
(very much, infinitely),
whatever they are,
are better than the results
of not having shown
that you care about my existence.
Because what experience says
is that it is much worse to not have it
said,
done,
or been.

MY CONGRATULATION (FIRST PART).

The beauty of the heart
of that lady in question
dissipates my reason
and accelerates rehab.

NEW SEASON.

This poem has the same spirit and rhythm as the song "Summer's Just Begun" from "Tinker Bell and the Great Rescue". I recommend listening to it before or during the reading.
And always, actually, although I leave that to the will of the people who read me.
Happy Autumn everyone, fairies and humans. 09/05/20.

New season,
the sun and moon spin and join in rotation.
Autumn has come on this day in the region.

The fairies do their work,
the trees change very slowly.
Flowers grow each in its space.

The blackbirds are singing again,
I can see life with a clear eye.
There is hope for another month.

Music fills the fall,
subtle changes in the environment.

Everything is preparing for one more year.

Only those who carry dust in their veins
know how to flow with the full moons,
and notice whenever People are close.

Nature changes,
renews and transforms.
And that is thanks to it being guided.

That white pigeon
today peeked through my window.
It's the transport they drive when they get near homes.

The time of certain legends has come,
the leaves fall even on the *hacienda*.
Soon it will be time to put the *ofrenda*.

Feeling the changes in the seasons
is simple if you have magic hearts.
Two full-featured faerie wings also help.

NOTES 4 & 5.

HAIKU OF THE BOOK.

This is *chicken soup*
(such a wonderful reading)
for the soul of all.

NOTE 6.

A BOOK TO TEACH ME TO…

I will understand
how not to suffer
being sensitive.

There is a book to read
about how to live
in an overly stimulating world.

The main reason I read Ted Zeff's books
is that I want to know how
to survive
stress, feelings and disasters.

There are many things to learn.
Most are supposed to be internal,
easy to apply.
I will proceed.

The Highly Sensitive Person's Survival Guide.

I've tried it on my own, in every thinkable manner.

Did it work my way?
The answer to that question varies
depending on the day,
but today, apparently, it's not possible.
That's why, when my efforts fail,
I search for (and fortunately find)
something to bring me back to my sensitive center;
a book to teach me to...
deal with my life
without losing myself,
to be sensibly realistic
both inside and out.

SILENCE.

Many times silence
is the best comrade
when what you want to say
is not really what you mean.

MY CONGRATULATION (EXTENSION).

Drives away all affliction;
works without vacillation.
Disposes of the discomfort,
looks for another solution
and accepts my condition.
She loves with great decision,
and treats me with compassion.
She's pure and beautiful emotion
while singing our song.

Changes the conversation,
assesses the situation.
Modifies by salvation,
to attract creation.

She stirs up passion
with her thinking and her action.
She moves position,

increases anticipation
by presenting every option.

Chooses every relation,
creates in her imagination.
She knows about stimulation,
and appreciates my intention.

Understands my emotion,
and trusts my intuition.
Uses every conversation
to grant a beautiful lesson.

And for that, for her expression,
for everything I mention
on every occasion...

For staying by my side with determination,
for never going down the path of my perdition,
for having faith in our connection,
for always counting on me and with my opinion.

For healing me without hesitation,
for knowing that I am more than an evaluation,
for remaining alongside me despite opposition,
for delaying the moment of leaving me with resignation...

And for thousands of other things, for the infinite love,
for each respiration...
for every second you give me of your attention...
because even now you care about my education...
for all the times you understand my reaction...

...my mother, great lady, biggest pillar of my life and vision...

...I write to give you today, and forever, my congratulation.

VERSES.

Present verses
for distant people.
I speak with poetry
for kind ears.
I sing with my soul
seeking to hear you.
I don't know if you hear me
but anyway
what I want
to do
(the only thing I know how to do,
the only thing I'm good at)
is to write you...
verses.
Verses of all kinds,
verses to feel
together.
All of us,
always,
everlasting,
together in (between) the verses.
Verses to tell stories,
verses for time to (not) pass.

Verses.
Verses that I hope will inspire you
to write your own
verses.

HAIKU OF NEW BEGINNINGS.

It has all vanished;
and so to write it once more
is the challenge now.

VERBOSITY FELT AT DAWN.

I lose me,
I find me,
I feel myself inside.

I move,
I settle,
I create my own memories.

Desires,
dizziness
and sleepless nights without nice dreams.

Meditated
dawn sunrises
and mornings of hopeful prayers.

Lost,
spoiled,
and a meaningless routine lived.

Action,

satisfaction,
and in the end, of all I love, destruction.

Creeping
desires.
Their pursuit
creates whole days of stuffy nose.

What is the point of wishing? What is it for?
What's the point of wanting?
If there's no love, maybe.

If you looked at me perhaps you could see
someone who just wants to understand.

Understanding, understanding.
How much pressure to understand!

If you listened to me you might hear
a *PAScual* sharing her feelings.

Perhaps if you watched me you would sense
my greatest conflict, during night and day.

They are already awake, now I must cease
expressing, for today, my verbosity.

NOTE 7.

UPLIFTING HAIKU.

Motivational
anticipation of love.
Can my heart feel it?

POETRY.

Dedicated to Julieta Ax, because one of the poems in her new book inspired me to write this.

This year I made it my goal
to read ten books of poems.
I don't know if I've read a couple,
or if that was last year already.

What I know is that words float in the wind,
and I don't know how to tell them I've changed.
It may be that they keep telling me
so many things I don't understand.

My light moves, changes.
It varies as the days go by.
I wouldn't know how to tell you all the secrets
that I light up when I look into the distance.

If there's one thing I know, it's that poetry hasn't lost its appeal,
but that time simply hasn't stopped.

So many words that come out of my fingers...
Of them, very few are in verse
as I tread the path of longing.
Looking to pierce that thick veil.

I am sorry to say that now poetry
is like the waves in the Mediterranean.
It appears only from time to time,
and I have to be attentive to feel it.

Which means it's not always there,
while the prose
oh, the prose,
is permanent
inside my mind.

I could talk about commitment,
but being a poet is something elusive.
I want to avoid repeating the same thing,
and therefore,
waiting,
seeking
the understanding of the muses
and of time,
I say goodbye to this art,
although only for a moment.

CYCLES.

Adversity makes flowers bloom.
Without frosts there can be no seasons.

DECEMBER 3RD.

Thursday.
Third day of December.

Today I saw Jack Frost
when he came to my window.
I know he wanted to greet me
(and say):
Winter is here!

I welcome the cold with joy
because it shows me
that I am still alive for
another year.

I have also seen a fairy
reflect her brightness on my screen,
and now
I understand that all is still underway.

It is the time of Yule,
of living the magic again.

The time to honor the dead

gives way to that of celebrating events.

In this month one hears
the tinkling of the bell.
And I, too, am able to see
the periwinkle flowers
and the winkle color that all illuminates.

Winter makes me think
of what awakens
when everything is asleep,
of the life that grows
in the harshest circumstances.
December makes me think
of festivals,
parties
and rituals.
Of beginnings and endings.
Of purposes fulfilled.
Of ice and cold, and also
of how, in the end,
we all end up falling.
Always.

Today I think about nature,
and how its intelligence
gives us the protection we need.
Today I think about the frost,
and how it protects us from freezes.
Today I think of all those
who shelter in a shell
waiting for the day
when they can come out again.

Today I think of traditions
and how myths
are just
truths that we have forgotten.

Today I am thinking about
snowflakes
and how the only year it snowed
was when we moved here
and brought the cold with us.

Today I am thinking
about Christmas trees,
and how fairies had to
change their homes
every time we humans
decided to cut them down.

Today I am thinking about
Mother Earth,
and how she changes and renews herself.

Today I am thinking about
Australia,
and how little by little it recovers.

Today I am thinking
about the north wind
(Boreas),
and waiting for him
to command
his sons
(the Boreads)

to carry the cold
wind
all over this hemisphere.

Today I am thinking
of Saturnalia,
and all the annual births
of the sun gods.
Apollo,
Helios,
Mithra
of Persia
and all the rest.
I'm thinking of Frey.
And that our
custom
of decorating
a Christmas tree
comes from Yggdrasil.
I think of Panquetzaliztli,
and that during that time
Huitzilopochtli was born.
I also think of Inti,
and that this
is a month
of renewal and rebirth.

Today I am thinking
that the change of season
is coming sooner and sooner.
That the Earth needs love
to keep spinning.

Today I am thinking
of the hundreds of memories
I have created,
and all the dreams
that have come true.

Today I am thinking
that you are still with me,
and how much I wish
that they were here too.

Today I think about
what Christmas
means
(to me).

I'm thinking about
the days left until
the winter solstice.

I'm thinking of giving thanks
for everything I live,
and I think about toasting
to all the new friends.

I'm thinking
(I'm thinking about this a lot)
that I really want to celebrate.
I want to celebrate life,
friendship,
food,
music

and family.

Winter is here
to remind us
of the importance of change
and that everything rises and springs again.

Yule, Christmas,
call it what you will.
Just realize
that one year ends
and another begins.

Happy winter!
Happy Advent!
Happy new beginning!

EVENTS OF THE MOMENT.

The human being
is reflected in space.
The darkness within
is lit up by the stars.

WHY I SIGH.

Too many things to explain...
and too few things to say.

Too many things to talk about
when life is complicated.

Too many things I want to tell
and little confidence to share.

Too much life to explore
and feelings I don't know how to define.

Too many sighs to let out
because I wish to coincide.

RESERVE POEM.

If one day I don't know what to say,
if one day I don't feel like writing...,
this little poem will save me from myself.

IMPORTED AND DETERMINED.

To import, according to how it's been defined,
is not so much about liking, with or without reason.
No; it's about something much deeper.
To import is to bring in something external.
Believe it.
Someone important is a being that, being other,
you bring to yourself.
Importing is not a thoughtless act.
It is a right, a choice.
It appears once and no longer fades, it's fixed.
When you care about someone it's not a
logical process,
either.
This is why there are so many people who are afraid
that someone will destroy their control.
Importance cannot be chased quickly,
it is a feeling
that is like wine:
you understand it better over time,
after the impulses
it becomes mature.

And that is when someone, loving,
is transformed.
And begins to value privates and senses.
When importing, we decide.
When we care, we open up.
And that turns us into our best version,
towards the truth of our heart.
And that is why, imported,
we become determined.

NOTE 8.

FOR MY GUARDIAN ANGEL.

It's more than your green eyes,
it's more than your black hair,
even though I do go crazy for
the combination.
It is more than having seen you with braces
and now beautiful without them.
It's more than that, I promise you.
It's more than your new haircut
(I'm glad
you listened
to me about the middle part)
and liking you in makeup.
It's that you are my guardian angel,
you accompany me on the trip.
This car
may not have
seat belts,
but that has never mattered to you;
although sometimes we have collided
and we no longer talk as much,
you are always by my side.

Nothing and no one compares to you, BFF.
Do you want to know why?
We met at a gymkhana
more or less
eight years ago.
I was practically using
my new scooter
for the first time.
My father helped me with the games.
(Oh! How innocent we were.)
You see, you were there that day,
and even though I hardly remember anything
about the date,
I remember admiring you
as soon as I saw you.
I still remember when you were
a girl
with whom I messaged
by email.
I remember, animalflor.
I remember our friendship
from
then.
I remember the WhatsApp groups.
I remember I didn't even know how to use it,
at all.
I remember that for as long
as I can remember,
you've been there.
I remember the T-shirt
of Stitch's girlfriend
that my parents bought me
at Disneyland Paris.

I remember you used
to wear headbands.
I remember you wanted to help me
with everything, and you still do.
I remember that you always knew
(and you know)
what I wanted and what I needed
before I asked you.
I remember...
Oh, sure.
I remember *Malory Towers*,
do you remember, Angie?
I even made you a bookmark
braided
with green
and white wool
(Nostalgia...
I made many back then,
and whenever I look at them
they remind me of the girls we used to be).
There are things that I remember
and others that I don't,
but I will always remember that it was you
who suggested going to watch *Coco*.
I will never thank you enough,
Ángela,
believe me.
We saw it in the theater,
you, my father and me.
As well as
Cinderella
and *Del Revés (Inside Out)*.
I remember buying

T-shirts that matched.
And giving you one,
do you still have it?
I remember playing with your friends.
I remember taking that strange train
to Llanera and back to the fair.
I remember lots and lots of things of ours.
I remember seeing you so many times.
I remember going shopping.
I remember sitting at the table
of the restaurant that closed,
(almost) all those afternoons.
I remember when you came to Warner Park
with your classmates.
Many years have passed,
but I remember.
I remember
that you have always liked
animals
and country life,
and I remember that you always knew
that I am terrified
of dogs and cats.
I fondly remember
our book exchanges
and that sometimes you did not finish them
by the time we saw each other
once more.
I remember.
And if I remember
so many things,
it's thanks to you, my friend.
You made my tweens

so much less lonely.
You have been with me every step
of the way
and you have helped me
want to
walk it.
I thought I had other best friends
but none compares to you,
and in the end,
disappointed with others,
I always come back to you, because you love me
in the best way
that two friends
can love each other.
You have endured me telling you
everything when I was fighting
with my parents,
and I know that if I need to,
I can text you again.
You have supported me in every *fascinsession*
and that still now fills me with emotion.
You have read La visita de Héctor Rivera
and I know that you have also read some
of my poems.
I have shared
the great milestones
of my life
with you.
And even now that I'm
across
the
country,
you're still close.

Our relationship is strange.
We can go months without talking
and yet one day talk again
as if no time had passed.
I write many
verses
about how I have changed
and how everything changes
over the years.
Perhaps one of the reasons
why our friendship
comforts me so much
is that we continue to treat each other just
as great
although nothing in our lives is
the same as when we met.
Nothing and no one compares to you,
and I know you will be a great psychologist.
How am I sure, you say?
Because you are a great person
and it is a blessing to be able to call you
bestie.
Nothing and no one compares to you,
and never will,
because even when
we only talk
about astrology
(or music),
you make me feel loved.
Nothing and no one compares to you,
because you always remind me
and remember me.
Nothing and no one compares to you.

Good luck in your adult life,
I promise that I will accompany you
for as many years as I can
(as long as you want me by your side).
I love you very much, friend.
Happy coming of age!
Thank you for being part of my life.
I've seen you grow
and mature,
now it's time to see you blossom.
Thank you for all our friendship,
Angie.
You are my guardian angel.

NOTES 9 & 10.

HAIKU TO THE RAINBOW.

Today the rainbow
tells me the truth within all.
Everyone is light.

STRENGTH.

Strength of verses,
uncertain places,
explored by letters
that carry my breath.

Strength of the wind
that brings contentment
out of your beautiful
poetic pieces.

Strength of attempt
to express your moment
before the screen full
of new possibilities.

Dedicated to C. M. Pérez, who as @LunadePrimavera354 wrote beautiful poems on the internet. I recommend reading her works, she is a featured author on the WattpadPoesiaES profile and one of her poetry collections inspired me to write this.

CHRISTMAS FOR ME.

Yule, first day
(December 20),
I participated in a radio program.
Yule, second day
(December 21),
we saw (lived) the winter solstice.
Yule, third day
(December 22),
we made cocoa gingerbread cookies.

Yule, fourth day
(December 23),
when we are going to set up a game.

On the fifth day
(December 24)
I will publish a new poem.

Yule, sixth day
(December 25),
I will practice Christmas syncretism.

Yule, seventh day
(December 26),
we will sing some Christmas carols.

Yule, eighth day
(December 27),
we will play with the gift as a family.

Yule, ninth day
(December 28),
I will be thankful for every moment.

Yule, tenth day
(December 29),
I will review my list of resolutions.

Yule, eleventh day
(December 30),
I will connect with the Universe.

Yule, twelfth day
(December 31),
we will eat raisins at two o'clock.

Yule, thirteenth day
(January 1),
ends and begins in 2021.

HOURS OF SLEEP.

It's not insomnia,
it's not anxiety,
there are just too many
thoughts
running
through my mind.
That's the reason I don't sleep.
That is why,
as much as I
want
to fall asleep,
sometimes
(almost always)
I have a hard time.

Maybe falling asleep at midnight
is becoming a habit.
Maybe I get up
too early
for my own good.
Maybe this is not sustainable
over time...

I WISH...

I wish you both were here.

I imagine it.
Me listening to your laugh
(which I can't imagine)
and telling you that it
is not really high-pitched,
not as much as you think.
You calling me by that beautiful nickname
you've given me,
and me blushing with happiness
because no one else calls me that.
I wish I could feel your breath close
and hold one of your hands in mine.
I don't know what they are like, smooth or rough,
big or small.
There is so much I don't know about you!
I'd like to see you,
even with so many masks you wear on your skin
to protect yourself
from something I can't understand.
I'd like for you to kneel beside me
and for us to ride my motorized unicorn

(because yes, there is room).
I would like to wrap you in my arms,
those that I sometimes cannot control,
and give us such a hug
that disappears the more than seven thousand kilometers
that separate us.
I would like to show you my house
and tell you, with hundreds of words,
what each corner means to me.
I would like to chat with you
on WhatsApp
while we are in the same place,
and know what tone of voice you use
to call me Annita.
I would like for you to tell me
(in person)
where in America
are you going to go when you can leave Cuba.
I would like for you to be able to understand me
just a few inches away.
I'd like for you to tell me what is it like
the place where you live
and run alongside you to show you quickly
(at five miles an hour)
why it does matter.
I would like to show you all the secret places
of my surroundings
and ask you which is your favorite butterfly
(mine is the white one, of the cabbage).
I would like to show you a beautiful sunset
one of those that are, here, the house specialty
and laugh together when the sky turns
scarlet.

I would like to know what is the touch
of your cheek
(I have a great longing for it)
and what is the smell of your presence
in my environment.
I would very much like
to know what color
your smile becomes
when you think about this.
I would like to know what
you really think of me,
and to observe your eyes
(know if they shine)
and how your face changes
when you think of me
without my knowing.
I would like to
catch you off guard,
and to have you express out loud
everything you say to me by text.
I would like you to read me aloud,
to go through my pages
as if I were an open book.
I wish you would tell me
(really)
what makes you be like Wanda.
And I would also like us to be free
as only two signs of Aquarius can be
(although our birthdays
are far apart
on the calendar).
I would like for you to ask me,
and that I could answer you.

I know you. You know me,
one doesn't need powers to read minds.
(But if necessary I have them, believe me.)
I would like to feel good.
I would like to know that you don't judge me,
not even when we're close.
I would like to go for a stroll around the place
and finally feel what freedom is.
I wish a plane would fly over our heads.
Then you could calm my fears
because I would already be living a dream.
We would cross the North Atlantic,
and I would feel great knowing
that your flowers bloom
during the same season as Spanish cacti.
I would like to show you each plant, and the trees.
Perhaps you would stand still
seeing that I express
appreciation
so strongly.
You may not think you're brave,
but to me you're so resilient...
that sometimes I wonder if I could withstand your life.
And the answer is always no.
I don't know if you would put up with mine,
but I don't care, because I'm positive.
You give me the feeling
that if you get close to me, I will be protected.
I would like to show you that here there's WIFI everywhere.
I would like to go to the mountain with you
and show you the wonder of having the world at your feet,

since I don't like the beach.
I would like to know how your handwriting is
on paper
and for us to write each other's names,
both in letters and in runes.
I would like to show you the truth
of my conditions
(which can be gifts or curses).
I would like for you to see me in every possible way,
with your keyboard in your eyes to (de)scribe me.
I would like to give you a million stories,
make many books present for you to read
and keep them all in your soul.
Soul that expresses itself everywhere
and that
I would like to make happy
so that you never feel
the need to say goodbye to me.
I would like to show you how important you are in my life
and that you make me want to live it
because you are always there on the other side,
although sometimes your Cuban internet
makes you take a long time.
I would like to give you a lot of things.
I want to make you
feel
the magic
of my ideas.
I wish
you could
believe
again.
But I think that, for once,

I would only like to make
that beautiful photo come true.

I will probably disappoint you when you meet me,
because the real me is shown only behind the screens.
Perhaps you would not even recognize
in me the one who says so many beautiful words to you.
But
you know what?
I do not care.
(And you have taught me to be able to say it honestly.)
I care about you so much that it doesn't matter.
It would be worth the fear.
(Yes, fear. Whoever coined the phrase
"It's
worth
the risk"
didn't know me.)
It would be worth the fear of disappointing
myself
for not knowing how to give you
what you need,
for not meeting your expectations.

Because I want you both to be here so much
that just one hour
person-to-person, or maybe all three together,
would be worth risking what we've got so far.
For just one minute
making my dream come true
(just Another Minute With You, with both),
making that drawing come true,
I wouldn't mind ending up wrecked

in an Inevitable manner
(as long as I'm not Behind the Glass of the smartphone,
as long as someone else listens with me to
The Voice of Silence)
as long as it is Reality & *not* Reflection,
as long as I feel you Another Instant,
so as not to live in a world Tortured
with The Double Torture of you not being by my side,
constantly thinking about the Memory
of what Was Love
(*philia*).
Although
"Maybe writing is just
one
of the ways
to
organize madness"...
Melting my Frozen Heart,
I make the following Silent Declaration
in this, my Dear Diary
in the form of a poetry collection,
which also holds my own version of
The King's Farewell:

In all the alternate universes, in all the nows, in every moment,
I yearn to be constantly overstimulated
by your combination of Fire & Gunpowder.

TOO LONG-AWAITED ENDINGS.

"Poetry is the feeling that is left over from the heart and comes out of your hand." Carmen Conde. *Dictionary of Quotations.*

Oh, how I wish I could cry!
Tears would be a relief now.
But, treacherous, they cloud my sight
and prevent me from freeing myself from longing.
Sometimes words are not enough.
Especially when they are what has caused
me to feel such an emptiness in my mind,
such that it's impossible to overcome it.

Sometimes words
do not solve anything
when it is the lack of response
what causes the nothingness.

Sometimes the cessation of an existence
is way worse than indifference.

Sometimes you know that someone
is not replying
because they are planning
how to break your heart
into thousands of pieces.

Haste
is not a good adviser
when we have to respect
the decision that has been made.

I do not know what else to say;
I only started writing
because
I can't bear to know
that it's over.

Everything in life are cycles
and this one, right now,
is ending.

THESE WALLS CRY OUT YOUR NAME.

Is it possible that I forget
about me,
about you,
about *us*,
if these walls
are not here
to surround me with your love,
to whisper your name
and sing me one of your songs
when I feel down,
so that the memories come
endless, always everlasting,
and to see you, all of you, once more?
Because the only thing that's special
about these walls
(the only special thing this house has)
is that they cry out your name,
your joy,
your being
and your presence
in every square inch.

ANY PASCUAL

And that is, is in part,
the perennial way that I have found
to recall you;
remember you.

Because you were here,
you were in this place,
not only in my head
or in my heart
and its beat,
you touched this place,
we walked through the hallways.
And everything,
here,
everything,
lovingly,
loving me and
knowing the immense
need
I have
of memories,
does everything it can
to keep you in my mind;
cries out your name.

BONUS

JOY OF BEING.

Joy of being.

Fifteen thousand five hundred twelve times
I wondered
what it would be like if you were next to me
(just once).

Fifteen thousand five hundred times
I answered myself
that I don't know, if it were to happen...
(for once).

And yet yesterday,
thinking about you again,
I realized
that you are happy like this.

The other eleven times
I imagined it
in great detail
to

see you well.

And although I only see you
in my mind,
I enjoy every moment
of noticing that it is us.

And when I think
of all the verses
that I have written to you
(all the verses that I will never stop
writing for you,
all the words I wish
I could say to you),
everything is summed up
in
a
single
sentence:
I want to know that you are happy
(preferably
while
you think
of me).

And although I would prefer
that you were here,
it is enough for me
to talk to you
and to know
that you are happy.

ANY PASCUAL

*For each and every one of the
people
important in, of, my life
from whom the distance
separates me.*

TOO MUCH WIND.

Wind, please,
stop scaring me with your howl.
I beg you, Zephyrus, Notus,
relax your spirit, if only a little.
Please, air,
let me calm down.
Mighty Nature,
become harmonious now;
bring peace and tranquility,
if it can be.
I want to flow with the cycles,
but I am much more serene
than the twenty-two miles
per hour
of the wind
gusts
on the eve
of my solar return.
It's too intense,
I'm too in the wind,
in too deep.
There has been wind from the beginning,
but too much

disturbs me, I don't focus
and I don't know how to stop it,
the Climate
Control
Magic
is not working.
I love the flow of the moments,
the Air and the Elements,
but this is too much,
too much time.
Too much wind.

SUMMARY OF YOU AND ME.

You changed my life, and now I can finally say
that I have written a poem dedicated to you.

Every day and night of my life, always,
always carry your feelings.
For in three days and two nights,
you taught me how to live.

February 2nd, the day I heard from you.
February 2nd, you helped me sleep.

November 1st, the day you came to me (the day I met you).
The initial words: "Do we know each other?" "You don't know me, but I do know you."
I felt so much
that words cannot describe it.

November 1st, the night you left,
the night you missed me,
and the night you came back.

The night I dreamed what was conveyed,
the memories of your living past.

November 2nd, a day that I have yet to explore,
to remember.

HAIKU OF HOPE.

Dedicated to my mother. Thank you for still being with me this September 11th. Love you.

Your encouraging
rainbow of motherly love.
The light of a smile.

PLATONIC.

What is platonic love?
I haven't known
(unrequited) love
for a long time.
I've long been aware that I love myself.
It's been long since I don't need anyone to love me...
unless it's you, skin to skin.
My platonic love.
He who should not be.

I can't talk about my friends...
I can't talk about my family...
nor am I going to talk
about the souls connected to mine
(because even if no one else sees them,
and everyone thinks it's platonic,
I know it's a real,
conscious,
and reciprocated love,
a love that I have taken care
of making clear
that it's not romantic,
because I live it and I have felt it)...

since none of these three kinds of love
is, in the least,
unidirectional
or strange.

Nor am I going to talk about the love of my life
(which is myself),
although sometimes I do rely on my ideas
to love me.

No.
If I want to talk about platonic love
I can't talk
(nor do I intend to)
about none other than you.

It's been a long time since I've known the feeling
of knowing that I'm idealizing,
that the other person doesn't even know me
and that the words I dream of
(the words I hope to hear from your lips)
are nothing more than inventions
that my brain creates
to make me fall asleep every night...
Unless, of course, it is about you.

For me, words have power,
you know,
and names are like spells
that open
futures.
In your case, the four letters of your name
create,

ANY PASCUAL

if said
out loud,
a world that no one
would want to live in.
As much as it is about you.

I have long since
decided
not to be the hunter,
but the prey.
To let everything come to me,
and let love reach me if it's true,
if it brings sincere words.
To stop chasing something futile
and be what is longed for.
I've decided long ago that I don't want
what your chaos can cause if we get together,
and even so, dear,
being able to say that I don't love you,
I keep looking and searching for you
everywhere,
in every way,
without expecting you.

You have turned me into the hunter who hunts
a game piece made of air,
the one who would be unhappy
if at some point she actually hunted you.

You have turned me into that hunter
who instead of being clever and resourceful
sets traps only behind herself
so that she can't get out

of this vicious obsession.

I have asked you
several times
to stop pretending,
to eliminate hope
and to go where I cannot reach you.

And still I search for you,
every night, every day,
every moment of idleness
that later brings me misery
knowing that, here, you have never been.

And even though I don't think
love is based on that,
I've already said I don't love you,
although I do want you.

So,
my heart
beats too fast,
and your smile doesn't stop it,
not even when you speak
and tell me everything
I don't know how to escape from,
everything I do know
I don't want to avoid.

Though I know that true love is eternal,
what I feel for you is temporary
and depends on you,
it is in your court

if you want
this deception of love
to remain for days, months,
years,
or more than a century.
And since you don't know
that it depends on you,
this is going to go on
like this
until
more summers change.

I lose you when I wake up,
because I can only talk with you alone.
Sometimes, when it pleases you
to please me,
you manifest yourself
with the form
and the voice
that you know captures my attention
(and my libido, if we're being honest).
When to you and only you it appeals,
you answer my nightly call,
slipping into midnight dreams
that fade when the morning
reminds me
that it's platonic,
that you're not there.
But it all seems so real
when...
Never mind.
It's not like I'm going to explain it.

What I am going to do is not the question I ask myself.
I know exactly what to do to express
myself when you leave my body frustrated,
realizing that I have imagined
everything
on my own
and alone in my room.
I write it, I always write it,
as I am writing now,
to get you out of my system
and at the same time keep you in memory.

What I am going to be is not the question either.
I can't imagine what would become of me
if it hadn't been for you,
although
I know you really had
nothing to do with it.
I even less want to think
(although
I often think about it with pleasure)
what would become of me with you,
if my fantasies were
becoming true.
And the when,
the when has never been an option.

I awoke from my latest
delusional dream
knowing that you are platonic
and with verses in my thoughts.
Verses that,

luckily
(or unfortunately, depending on how you look at it),
are not exactly these.
I no longer remember what I wanted to tell you,
although I do remember that last dream we dreamed.

Ah, okay,
part of it
was this.
What do you want me to tell you, darling?
In another dream a faceless person
asked me how you were possible.
How could it be that someone platonic
was so necessary to be stronger.
Why I had put my hopes in you
when the yearning would never come true.
And I couldn't answer that,
but I feel it.

The real doubt that has no answer
is:
Why?
Why, given that our union
not only causes distress, not only is not possible,
but it shouldn't be,
why knowing that it is platonic,
why knowing
that you bring evil and that you are crazy,
that you are still only for a few,
that you have fallen to the lowest,
and yet you are infinitely more powerful
than me,
that you are on an absolutely higher level,

I continue and continue and continue
wanting you,
and although it is forbidden
I continue
seeking you, needing you,
desiring you?
Why you, my platonic?

I THINK SO.

How to say nostalgia
without defining nostalgia?
Is it that feeling
I feel when I wish
I was in times past,
like a kind of melancholy?
Is it perhaps a word
with nine letters,
three syllables,
et cetera,
an insubstantial noun,
but too irreplaceable
to be confused
with something else?
Is she as defined
by the Oxford English Dictionary?
Or is she perhaps the most
perfect material for any poem?
Even I, a thoughtful character,
never utter that
feeling
out loud.
Nostalgia, nostalgia, nostalgia.
What does nostalgia evoke in me?

Is that what I feel when I hold you
close?
Or is that something else?
They are the memories that poetry evokes,
that reason why I try not to
feel so lost.
But nostalgia, like everything else,
is elusive.
She disguises as her sister, longing,
during the day,
and at night she goes out locked up,
if that is possible,
without moving an inch,
without disappearing,
without bringing relief,
in the form of tears.
Tears for all I've lost.
For all I have known
and, at the same time,
will never experience.
For all that is in my heart
that no one has ever seen,
nor will attempt to comprehend;
for all the hidden reasons
even I don't understand.

I don't know what it is for you,
but for me it's this...
That word I don't utter here,
because it's like it's killing me.
Nostalgia.
Yes, I think that's it.
I think that's nostalgia.

ON HER DAY, FOR MY MOTHER.

Regardless of the oppositions
she will encounter in tons
because of her past and present choices,
she supports me in my decisions
and concretizes them with valuable actions.

Infinite waves of emotions
we feel being the two together.
There are no definitions for you,
because you and I, Mom, are one.

This is one of those days to say to you,
in a light hug, bold, as always,
that beautiful phrase which is of daughter and mother;
that goes, today too, "Yes it's possible!"

SAFE AND SOUND.

Safe and sound,
alive and kicking
I go self-inspiring
even if life
is not,
really,
as I would like it.

Safe and sound here
the words don't want to come out,
my feet won't walk,
and my disease
(the one that makes me breathless)
won't fly away
and
leave.

Safe and sound another day I make it.
And yet,
everything else is so ephemeral
that I try to hold on to verses
without any meaning
just to preserve the inspiration

that slips through my fingers
every time someone else goes fearlessly on
to conquer the whole world,
or maybe just one live.
All that,
sempiternal.

Safe and sound I am,
although there is no
(eternal)
salvation
and Health is a dream
yet unmanifested
in these lungs breathing
breathlessly.
Simply,
for that which I give to all
and all that everyone gives me,
paraphrasing Donés,
perhaps,
maybe,
life, even if I suffer, is worth
my while
if I can be honest
and recite one more Thursday.

NOTE 11.

GÜELITO.

Güelito,
today is your birthday
and therefore I dedicate this poem to you.
I already wrote one for my grandmother;
today I couldn't miss yours.
You like nature,
and you never close your heart.
You love the land,
and solving problems.
You often ramble
and relax by walking for a long time.
You plant in the garden,
and your arms are always open.
You greet me every time I come over,
and bring a smile to my face every time I see you.
You always find a way to help
everyone you come across.
You have a very kind soul,
even more than your skilled hands.
There is so much you have taught me
that talking about you fills me with pride.
That is why I'm writing this to you today,
because even though I don't always tell you,

I love being with you.
Every time I hear you talk about the past
(something you do from time to time),
I can imagine those years.
Even though you don't know much about technology,
I know that in other things you have mastery.
I learn something from you every day.
You always tell me what I didn't know.
Thank you for always taking us in,
and lending us a hand
with what we need.
I've already congratulated you, but I want to do it again,
so now, on this twenty-eighth day,
I can only say, like every January:
Very happy birthday, grandad!

FEAR.

Watch out that goes!
I go.
Fear
to withdraw
that I know.

Sea eyes!
I think.
Fear of letting time
slip away.

Dark circles of chance!
Unsettled.
Way to look,
absent.
Fear.
My *depends*.
Fear.
My cause,
desire
to live
(or maybe to leave it at that),
if you look closely.

In losing,
in feeling,
in leaving,
in loving
and crying
without fear.

Because fear,
just like that
pain
of what I once lived without meaning,
of what I once felt without living it,
is what might help me.
Because that fear that helps me overwrite,
that one that helps me put it all into perspective,
may be serving me somehow.

Maybe fear isn't always bad.
It could be that fear is my ally.
It could be that fear makes me let go of my ego.
And although I fear thousands of experiences,
thousands of people,
what I do
to counteract
and control the terror I live with
is what makes me have free will;
fear is what I need.

Fear is what keeps me alive.

Because as I once said,
without fear, we are not human,

and *Blogger6Fowl*'s sensitivity is based on it.
On that fear is another form of suffering,
another thing I repel.
Another thing I avoid at all costs when I can.
But I can't always do so.
And what do I do then?
Be afraid of fear?
Yes, I do; I admit I get paralyzed.

But, as Priscila Gibert
today has taken upon herself
to remind me,
I once made a poem saying:
"Sensitivity,
pain,
reminds us that we are alive".
And now I would add:
Fear
is a reminder
that there is another way.
There is always,
always another way.
That's why we have survived.
All has always been
about the balance
between love,
desire,
and fear.

AUTHENTICITY.

I can't tell you how to do it.
There are no shorter paths, or shortcuts either.
It's just you and the feeling of the moment.
Oh, and then comes the ignorance.

I honestly have no idea.
I don't know what I'm doing.
I don't know if I'm worth it
or if this will seriously help anyone.

The only thing I know is what I want.
The only thing I know is that I can.

Asking yourself "Why not?"
has exactly the opposite effect.
All those tactics do not help me,
because what I want is... to love.

Love my trait.
Love my sensitivity.
Love my poetry,
love my truth.

How can this serve any purpose?
I don't have the answer.
I don't have the door,
I don't even know it.
I have neither reason,
nor authority nor independence.
I don't even have enough self-esteem
to deal with the losses.

I am being very honest.

What I do have is fear.
But that's a subject for another poem.

I don't know why I'm creating this book.
I just want to be sensitive,
please people,
and be happy
enjoying that we are finally visible.
For us not to be afraid
to express our opinion.

I'm going too slow,
slower than I'd like.
I want for this to make you feel empathy,
and for that every word has to be perfect.

Why do I count the syllables?
What about the spaces?
The answer is on each blank line.

I'm Highly Sensitive.

That doesn't justify everything.
Understand me,
please.
I'm not trying to hide
behind a justification.

Quite simply, our desire for peace
makes us conscientious beings.
Being aware
of the details,
perfectionism is a lurking entity.

I don't take well the control,
the deadlines
or the weight of the process.

I want to be useful!
I want the world to know me!
I want to be able to say
that being different is not wrong.
That to be sensitive is normal.

I want to say we have talent.
We just have to trust ourselves much,
much more.

Don't make decisions based on ego impulses.
Not even if it is to pay for this.
That doesn't work.
I tell you from experience.

What works is listening.

Attend to other people,
seek out experts
and use your ability to relate.
Listen to your body.
What are you telling yourself?

Taking risks is not simple.
The easy part is to be authentic.
Sharing that with the world takes time.

Now, breathe.
You know what you feel.
A lot of times, that's all we know.
And it's okay.
Speak sincerely,
stay silent when you want to shut up.

What the world thinks matters, yes.
But have you ever wondered what you think of yourself?
That's what will get you there.

You don't have to be like anyone else.
You have no reason to follow the advice of others.
You are you, and that's what matters.

HSP, human being, I am your friend.
Between these pages,
you can be whoever you decide.
Absolutely all your craziness is welcome.

I am so too, I am like you.
I am intuitive, sensitive and introverted,
and I am also positive, kind and alive.

I also go through dark periods.
Sometimes I'm lost, the pain doesn't go away.
But you can live with it.
And in the end that enriches the soul.

I don't know what it is I am doing,
but I do know it is pretty.
And writing it is helping me.

There is a sparkle in you, I assure you.
Even if no one sees your light, it exists.
Just by existing you are already someone.
Just by living, you're already valuable.

I don't know if anyone will read these words,
but to me, they make sense.
Don't wander through life in fear and for no reason.
Find your own personality.

Maybe no one has told you before,
so it's my turn to tell you.
I know what you're capable of.
I see who you really are.
And that person deserves to be.

Live.
Keep going.
Give that sense to what is happening to you.
Be different and learn to appreciate it.
Feel, for it is your great gift.

Sensitivity is a gift.

Let's make the most of it.
Go out into the world, I support you.
You can switch if you so decide.

Embrace how you are,
embrace your presence in the present.

Doing your best
is not striving to overcome yesterday.
The best way to do it is to know yourself
and understand that every day is different,
and that you are not the same person
you once were.
The best way to do it
is to incorporate your own
energy
into your life
and start being real
day after day.

The best way to do it is to love your sensitivity,
be that as it may, without barriers.
That's what I like most about being HSP.
It's something we cannot and do not want to avoid.

Authenticity.

ACKNOWLEDGEMENTS.

I thank Life for my talents and the Universe for my circumstances.

Thank you to my readers for buying this book and reading it through.

Thank you to my parents, for showing me what infinite love is and for giving me so many opportunities to explore my sensitivity. And also for inspiring many of my best poems. I know that life is not always easy for you, nor is it for me; the three of us are in this together. Our paths are linked for life, and I rejoice, because I need you to grow. Even though sometimes it doesn't seem like it, I appreciate what you give me day in and day out, both the joys and the hard times and reality buckets. I am who I am because you are here with me every step of the way. I love you.

Thanks to Priscila Do Amaral Gibert, for everything. Especially for the afternoons spent talking about butterflies, trees and tulips. Thank you for making the covers of this book perfect, just the way I like. Thank you for the many sketches and for putting up with me when I asked for another one. It's an honor to see my ideas captured in your strokes. You are the best. I really appreciate your love, your support and your constant words that always make me feel. I am sure that one day you will publish a great book and it will be a pleasure to read it as you have read all my poems. Thank you for your friendship, *min kjaere*. I love you, Miss. Smile at João for me, and continue to be yourself, because you are a woman who's magic. Always. I am happy that you are part of my team; your talent is a blessing. I get better every day thanks to having you in my life. I love everything you do. I support you.

Thank you to author Dr. Elaine N. Aron for helping me recognize myself as part of a collective, to give a name to what I feel, to understand myself. All this poetry exists thanks to *The Highly Sensitive Person*. Your work changed my life, and I thank you for all the blessings that being an HSP has brought me. I consider you a sage, and with this book I am sharing my gift to increase awareness and recognition of sensitivity. Thank you infinitely, from the bottom of my heart. Let's feel, for the world needs us.

Thanks to Ted Zeff, for representing highly sensitive men, for his book, his experience, his knowledge, and his skills and techniques. I dedicate a poem to him because his words helped me at a difficult time. I hope that even more HSPs can benefit from what I have learned by reading *The Highly Sensitive Person's Survival Guide*.

Thank you to Carmen Conde. She is an inspiration to me, and I adore that when reading her poems I find a soul with so much to say, a kindred heart. I see myself reflected in her verses, and honestly I consider her a role model for me. If I could tell her anything, I would tell her that her words have shaped a poet. They have centered me and given me peace, because in a few words she has managed to convey what I have sought and found in this book, while writing and editing. I hope that by quoting that sentence I can help more people discover her feelings, her poetry. I believe I have done her justice. To you, to your art, and to your life. Thank you for sharing yourself with the world, and with several generations. RIP.

Thanks to the writer Julieta Ax. If I write poems, it's because your works have shown me the depth and personality of poetry. I admire you. You are a great writer who inspires and helps many people. Your books are some of the best poetry I've ever read. Thank you for influencing my art in such a positive way. Being different is wonderful, and expressing our feelings sincerely is even better. I learned that from reading you. You are a teacher to me, and I can relate to your verses. I'm your fan.

Thanks to Dante Verne. Your observations and advice have made this book better. Every time I recite one of my poems in front of you, you have the right words to motivate me and boost my self-esteem. You make me feel at home because I know you understand me. Thank you for your experience and patience. You deserve the best.

Thank you also to Ashley Lorenz, Priscila Gibert and Linda Simpson, for their help in editing and translating this book. You are more than precious. Keep carrying on!

To Furkan, for being the blue butterfly that flies alongside my own. I love you.

To Leah Garoz, aka scarlet rainbow snake diamond. You are my craziest friend. And that's saying a lot! I love you too much. Keep writing and shining. And may your career bring you all the happiness and success you deserve. You are amazing, and I'm so proud of you. Thank you for teaching me to love myself and to know how to say yes. Kisses, and a very big hug. I still hope to see you someday. Love, your little squirrel.

Thank you, Laura, for making me smile, for sharing paths with me and for being by my side when I started posting my writings on Wattpad. Love you in a friendly way.

Ángela, my guardian angel on earth, my best friend since forever. You are there whenever I need you, and I really appreciate your energy and you being my confidant. Wherever you are in the future, our hearts are together. You have my support to do anything. Thank you for everything, Angie. You're great.

To my internet friends.

To Aengus Murray, for your appreciation and for being a gorgeous person, for your purple hearts and for the comfort you give me; us meeting was no coincidence. I hope one day you learn enough Spanish to read all my poetry. I care and I believe in you.

To Jaylen. What can I say? You have helped me from day one. Thank you for the late night talks and for clarifying that I deserve me. I appreciate your faith in me, that you are willing to believe me even when I don't know what

I'm doing and my words make no sense. I adore your personality and I know you will do important things that will help the world. I appreciate you. Thank you for giving me hope and a desire to live. I want to be by your side for many more years, friend. To your success. I have a huge desire to meet you in person.

To Intern. You so deserve to be here, even if we no longer talk. Knowing you're on the other side makes me happier than you think. You give me peace. Thank you for letting me be myself and for never judging me, no matter how I behave. And also for helping me feel normal. You are honest, loyal, and affectionate. I hope you get everything you want. I couldn't have asked for a better friend with whom to celebrate my eighteenth birthday. I care about you, you're valuable and I'm glad you keep going. I am here for you at every stage, because I know who you are and I love it. Lots of virtual hugs!

To Matthias Ku, for being so wholesome, both inside and out. Thank you for your friendship, Matze.

To Tayveon, for being there when no one else had time, for your interest in getting to know me, for keeping me enthusiastic with your messages, and for always texting me at the right time. And for the blushing you've caused me with your compliments. I hope life fills you with happiness for all the joy you gave me. Thank you for every word we shared.

John, my Roué. Across time and space, you're an unexpected discovery. May we get together someday. Cheers!

To Kwame Nkuah Tawiah. I'm happy to have you. Your hugs and affection brighten my dark days. We care about each other, and that's awesome. Thank you for being there, because the distance disappears every time you make me blush: I feel you near. May my poetry reach your heart, as you reach mine. And may your book and your words bring lots of love and joy to many people, as you bring them to my life every day. You have talent, and you are lovable. I'm so proud of you!

To all the Discord folks. Thank you for being there and for giving me an easy and fun way to share my truth with the world. To Jaynlin for the reminders, to the MBTI Bakery community for the good times and the positivity channel. To each and every person in AstroBriggs for being even crazier than me, and for putting me in contact with love. I made it. This INFP did it. To the people in Write Your World, too, for being far more than words can say, and for such a virtual home. To Mira, for the words of support. To Jaime, for being solid and giving me so much care. To Lucía, for the times we almost met, and for Miley Cyrus. You know what I mean. To Benja, Tati, Andrés and the others, for being my virtual family. To everyone on the Percy Jackson server, for the roleplaying and for the craziness. It's been a great year. And to everyone I have ever shared my time, knowledge, and poems with, for always being kind to me. I love you all, Discordants. Even if I don't know all your names by heart.

To Leonid Blyum, because thanks to you my circumstances are better than anyone thought they would be. Thank you.

Thank you to Robert Kiyosaki, for teaching me so much and for showing me that education leads to prosperity. You are a huge influence on me. And to Fernando González, for your time and your constant desire to help. Hugs and lots of good vibes. Working with you on your book was a wonderful opportunity, and I am so very grateful that our paths have crossed. Blessings to you and your family.

A big thank you also to Om Elisayah Soham (and the Elisabeth Giner Foundation) and to María José Lladó (of Editorial Kolima) for believing in my talent and my future as a writer, and for offering me your help and resources in case I ever needed them. You were the ones who helped me imagine a time when I would consider myself "author of...", so long ago, when my poems were still just loose pieces scattered on various Internet sites and most of the poetry that makes up this book had not yet been written. Both of you, in different ways, turned a vague idea into something plausible and helped me see how my sensitivity could help the world. Thank you for your time and enthusiasm.

To Héctor, Imelda and Coco. You move me. Thank you for always remembering me. What matters is what matters, you have taught me to love. See you the next day, and when it's time. I am un poco crazy, and so happy to have met you! These five years alongside you have been the best. Thank you for being by my side and accompanying me wherever life takes me. I love you all, Mexicans.

Thank you to my maternal grandparents, María Josefa

and José Manuel, for your constant support and love. Grandma, thank you for the stories that inspired the poem I wrote for you. Thank you for always caring about me and for being the most loving grandmother in the world. I love you so much. Beauty. Grandpa, thank you for taking care of us and for doing whatever it takes to make sure we are okay. I cherish every minute you spend talking with me, and I fondly remember those days when you taught me to draw, at the dining room table or wherever. Thank you. Every time I visit you, I remember where I came from and where I want to return. *Puxa*!

Thanks also to my extended family and relatives. To my great-aunt María Jesús, for asking me to dedicate this book to her long before it was finished. To my many cousins on both sides, for the good times during my childhood.

To my great-grandparents. Because you couldn't miss. You are one of my greatest influences, and I love listening to your stories. To my Bisa, my great-grandma Natividad, for showing me that love does not only reside in memory. Thank you for every act of love and caring gesture you have given me and this family. To Peregrina, for being my example of determination and firmness, and for teaching me that there is nothing wrong with being proud of who one is, quite the opposite. I live your legacy. To Cándido, for your example and for passing on your good temperament to the next generations. I would hug you right now if I could. Thank you, because thinking about you calms me down. To my great-grandfather José Manuel, for making me see the other side of life, because you have to endure very hard times (and people) to get ahead. It's not easy to go on, but we do it because there's no other way. And to Silvio. Every time someone mentions you, I am moved. To me, you have been proof that everywhere, and in every family, there is someone good. Even though we only saw each other once, you are still important to me. You remain an example to follow. Thank you for the kindness you have always shown to everyone, in your own way, and for your positive influence on my family's character. We appreciate you very much. To Esperanza, for your life's deeds and stories. Thank you for allowing me to be here. And thanks also to my great aunt, my mother's godmother, Carmina. You always took care of others the best way you could. I really enjoy hearing about you. I love you all! I'm happy to call you family.

Thank you to the Wattpad platform and the entire team behind it for helping novice writers express their talent in an easy and dynamic way. My writing has benefited immensely from all the resources and possibilities that have been within my reach with just a few clicks. Being in constant contact with other readers and writers, and especially with a community of people who are already interested in what they are about to read, is a great help for any author. Without a doubt, I've found it very useful.

And therefore, I want to thank every person who has ever voted with a star on my works, taken the time to leave a comment, and/or added my creations to a reading list. In part, this book exists thanks to your attention and feedback. I appreciate each and every one of your words and reactions.

Thanks also to my followers on Instagram, both those on my personal account and those who follow me on the public one. As Blogger6Fowl, I have been sharing snippets of my poetry, my *fanfiction*, and some other writings. You have all been very generous with your hearts. And I thank everyone who likes the content I post on any_espiritual, both on Instagram and Facebook. A light hug for all. Thank you for your support.

To all those who have helped me share my message in videos, podcasts, interviews and conferences. To Luis and Kinga and Beatriz, to the whole Radio Creatividad team, to Laurent (double thanks) and Estela, to Shaila, to the Generation Z team, to Rich Dad Latino and all the Rich Women who have been so amazing to me, to Sencillez Plena, to Pymela and Guga, to Diversidad Literaria for publishing one of my haikus as part of their fourth collection... I have had many opportunities, and I am grateful for each and every one of them. Thank you for helping me learn by teaching!

And finally, thank you to the Muses. Thank you to my beliefs and my faith, for being permanent. Thank you to all the spiritual beings that are out there.

And thanks to Soira, my spiritual guardian angel, to my Innate, my Self, my soul and my intuition. I listen, talk, write and do. Thank you for constantly giving me light and messages so I can share them with the world. Thank you for always moving me towards my truth, because thanks to your guidance I live happily with this heart full of sensitivity.

NOTE 12.

ABOUT THE AUTHOR

Any Pascual

Any Pascual (born in 2004) is a writer, blogger, speaker and HSP. This teenager is a being of light, a soul whose purpose is to love, understand and convey love. Sensitivity is her second book. A poetry book in which she expresses her trait of High Sensitivity from her personal experience, in a creative, spontaneous and barrier-free way, with the aim of  helping to accept, understand and appreciate the greater sensitivity with which she and many other people live. If you find yourself reflected in any of these poems, if you are moved by any page, then this book has fulfilled its purpose.

Any has been writing and sharing her work for years on various platforms, including Wattpad (under the pseudonym Blogger6Fowl), her website anayany.com, and social media.

You can find her at anayany.com, @any_espiritual on Twitter and Instagram, and @anyespiritual on Facebook.

BOOKS BY THIS AUTHOR

Sensibilidad: Los Poemas De Una Adolescente Altamente Sensible

La sensibilidad no debe ser una maldición, cuando realmente es una gran condición.

Conjunto de poemas relacionados con la sensibilidad, en especial el rasgo de la alta sensibilidad.
Mi experiencia siendo PAS, en verso.
Un poemario para iluminar tu alma y envolverla en un gran abrazo. Para ayudarte a que transites tu propio camino, reconociendo el don que siempre has tenido.
Eso que necesitas pero no sabes nombrar. Hasta ahora.

AUTHOR'S NOTES

1. Carmen Conde (1907-1996) was a Spanish poet, narrative writer and teacher. The original Spanish quote was part of the Diccionario de Citas (Quotations Dictionary), and reads as follows: "La poesía es el sentimiento que le sobra al corazón y te sale por la mano". An official English version of her quote has not yet been found. This translation is my own.
2. This poem was originally titled "659 palabras más sobre sensibilidad", in reference to the amount of words the Spanish poem has.
3. "Servir y proteger" (Serve and Protect) is a Spanish soap opera about a police station in Madrid and the cases the officers investigate. It was on the public television from 2017 to early 2023, when this book was being written. The other TV series mentioned is called Acacias 38.
4. You can listen to the song on Youtube: Summer's Just Begun - Tinker Bell and the Great Fairy Rescue
5. This book has a playlist on Spotify! Listen here: Book Playlist.
6. This haiku is based on the book Chicken Soup for the Soul, by Jack Canfield, Mark Victor Hansen and Amy Newman.
7. This is an untranslatable wordplay based on the way my surname, Pascual, incidentally matches with *PAS*,

the Spanish equivalent of the acronym HSP.
8. In Spanish, the verb "importar" (to import) is also used to mean "to matter" or "to care". This poem, originally titled "Importados y decididos", plays with that.
9. It is an old personal pun that mixes fascination and obsession.
10. My first delving into serious writing, in which many of the poems in this book are based. This is a story of hope, memories, and a friendship that transcends everything.
11. I am referring to a renowned Spanish song, "Eso que tú me das" (What you give me) by Jarabe de Palo, whose singer was Pau Donés.
12. It's a reference to the song "Un poco loco", from the Disney/Pixar movie *Coco*.

If you enjoyed my poetry, feel free to leave a review on Amazon. Thanks for reading!

Printed in Great Britain
by Amazon